7

LEARN ABOUT
The Inventors

By Jennifer Burnap
Illustrated by Edward Blake

First published in 1994
by Anglia Young Books
Durhams Farmhouse
Ickleton
Saffron Walden, Essex CB10 1SR

Illustrations by Edward Blake

British Library Cataloguing-in-Publication Data

A catalogue record for this book is available from the British Library

ISBN 1 871173 31 0

Typeset in Futura and printed in Great Britain by
Redwood Books, Trowbridge, Wilts.

CONTENTS

Alexander Graham Bell
The Telephone

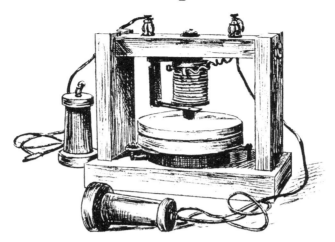

Alexander Graham Bell was born in Scotland in 1847. He was a very clever boy. He went to the Royal High School in Edinburgh where he studied music.

Alexander's whole family was very clever. Both his father and grandfather were professors. They taught deaf children to speak.

Alexander's mother was deaf too, so Alexander spent much of his spare time helping deaf people.

In 1870 a terrible thing happened to the Bell family. Both of Alexander's brothers died of tuberculosis. They had been very ill with bad coughs and they had found it hard to breathe. Alexander also had a bad cough and his parents were frightened that he too might die. They had some friends in Canada whose son Graham had been friendly with Alexander. Alexander even shared his name.

The Bell family went to Canada where the air was clear and fresh. It was very cold in winter, but Alexander began to get better.

While he was recovering he spent a lot of time reading. He was especially interested in the work that some scientists were doing.

One invention seemed particularly interesting. It was a tuning fork which worked by passing electricity through it. It could be used to make vowel sounds. Alexender didn't fully understand how it worked, but perhaps, he thought, it would be possible to send sounds through wire.

Alexander had already begun to understand that sound, and especially speech, worked by vibrations. If you held a dog's throat you could feel the vibrations when it growled.

He showed this to his friends.

If he could understand how we hear speech perhaps he would be able to teach deaf people in a better way.

After spending a year in Canada the family moved to Boston in America. Alexander eventually got a job there at the Boston School for the Deaf.

One day Alexander went to see an ear specialist to ask him to explain how our ears work.

The doctor was very interested in the young man's work and he showed him a model of the human ear. He explained that we have a small drum inside our ear and that sounds vibrate on it. These different sounds are sent like messages to the brain. The brain recognises the sounds as words which we learned when we were little.

Alexander was very excited. He began to work out how he could make electric sound on a wire that could be vibrated on a drum. He would call it a transmitter.

One day he had some visitors. They were called Mr and Mrs Saunders. They had a little boy called George who was deaf. Alexander had been teaching George to use sign language and he had made special games and books for him. The Saunders family were very grateful to Alexander and they offered to lend him a room in their house where he could work.

At first Alexander worked in the cellar but, later on, the Saunders gave him a bedroom too. Alexander was delighted. It was just what he needed for his experiments.

Alexander had heard a lot about a man called Samuel Morse who had invented a way of sending messages by electricity. Hundreds of miles of wire were strung across America and a pattern of dots and dashes were tapped out for the letters of words. It was all done by vibration.

Alexander decided that if Morse Code messages could be sent in this way, then so too could the human voice.

He wanted to develop this idea, but he still had to go to work every day at the School for the Deaf. He needed an assistant. One day he was in an electrical shop. He told the man who worked there that he was looking for someone to help him.

The shopkeeper suggested a young man whose name was Tom Watson.

Tom Watson agreed to work with Alexander in his spare time.

Tom knew a lot about electricity and the way it could be passed along a wire. Together he and Alexander set to work to build a speaking tube with a vibrating disk like the ear drum.

This then passed the sounds along the wire to another vibrating disk which turned the sounds back into words. Between the two disks was a bowl of sulphuric acid and a battery for the electricity.

Alexander believed that if you spoke into the speaking tube your voice would vibrate along the wires. It could then be picked up by the second disk.

On the evening of 10 March 1875, Tom arrived at the workshop.

'I think we're ready to test it,' Alexander said. 'You lay the wires up the stairs and join on the receiving disk.'

Tom did as he was told.

'Ready!' he called down the stairs.

Below in the cellar Alexander sat with the speaking tube and the part they called the transmitter.

His excitement made him clumsy. He fiddled with the equipment, anxious that it would work.

Suddenly he knocked over the cup of acid. It burned through his trousers onto his leg. It was very painful. He shouted for Tom.

'Tom! Come here quickly!'

'I heard you! I heard you!' Tom shouted as he rushed down the stairs. 'It works!'

Alexander forgot about his burned leg.

'Here,' he said 'You say something and I will listen upstairs.'

Tom sat down at the equipment. He couldn't think of a thing to say. At last he remembered a nursery rhyme.

'One, two, three, four. Who is knocking at my door? Five, six, seven, eight. How many cherries on my plate?'

Upstairs in his bedroom Alexander heard every word clearly. It was the most exciting sound he had ever heard.

He called the invention the telephone.

Now he had to see if it would work over a longer distance.

Alexander and Tom tried it between the neighbours' houses. The telephone worked well.

That summer they were in Canada at a place called Brantford. The two young men went to see the telegraph manager at the local office. Alexander told him about their telephone. He asked if they could use the telegraph line. The telegraph manager thought they were wasting his time.

How could the human voice possibly be sent over the wires which were used for Morse Code?

Alexander and Tom kept trying to persuade him.

'Think how famous you will be if it works,' they said.

At last he agreed.

Tom stayed in Brantford with the transmitter while Alexander travelled a hundred kilometres or so to a place called Paris. Here Alexander waited in a shoe shop. It was the evening of 10 August, 1876. A crowd of people gathered in the shop with him. A telegraph operator telephoned from Brantford and spoke to Alexander.

Alexander let some of the people listen to the voice from Brantford. They could not believe their ears! It sounded so clear!

Alexander's dream had come true! He had invented the telephone!

Today telephone wires cross over continents and cables are laid between countries on the ocean bed.

The design of the telephone has changed too.
Some telephones today are cordless and we can carry them around with us. Some telephones have televised pictures of the person we are speaking to.

The invention of the telephone has done more to bring the people of the world closer together than any other invention.

Ladislao Biro
The Ballpoint Pen

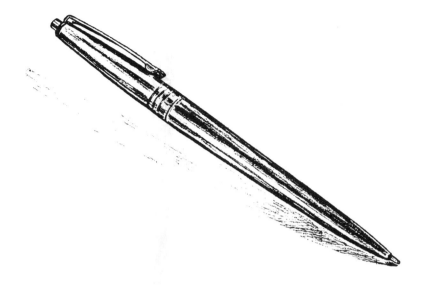

It is hard to write neatly with a fountain pen. The nib is easily damaged. You cannot write with a damaged nib.

The pen also has a little tube of ink inside it. Sometimes it leaks and makes a mess.

Once there was a man called Ladislao Biro. He lived in Hungary and he was a scientist. He liked inventing things. He invented a washing machine and a thief-proof lock, but we remember him because of his interest in pens.

Ladislao Biro was fed up with fountain pens. They broke too easily and they could be messy.

You always had to wait for the ink to dry so that you didn't smudge your writing.

Ladislao decided that what everyone needed was a quick-drying ink. He knew that it would be especially useful to printers. He was sure that artists and the people who make maps would also use it.

Ladislao's brother was a scientist too, and they often worked together.

They began to do some experiments with different kinds of ink. At last they found a mixture of inks that dried quickly. However, the new ink did not work as well in a fountain pen. It would not flow down the nib.

Ladislao began to design different kinds of nibs and the one that worked best was like a small metal funnel with a tiny ball inside it.

The ink flowed around the tiny ball and out through the hole at the pointed end of the funnel.

The person using the new nib was therefore writing with a ball at the end of a point.

Ladislao registered his invention and called it a ballpoint pen.

At that time the Second World War had just begun.

In 1940 Hungary was invaded by the German army and Hungary became a very dangerous place in which to live. Ladislao decided to leave. He went to Paris.

Unfortunately the Germans invaded France too and Ladislao wondered where he should go for safety. He had once met the President of Argentina when he was on holiday in Yugoslavia.

'If you are ever in my country do come and visit me,' the President had said.

Ladislao decided that this was a good time to visit Argentina.

He liked it so much that he became a citizen of Argentina.

He began to work on his inventions again and some of his friends gave him money to get started.

His family was still in Europe and Ladislao was very worried about them. He wanted to send them money so that they could escape like he had.

One day he met an Englishman called Henry G. Martin. Mr Martin was in Argentina on a business trip. The two men got talking and Mr Martin was very interested in Ladislao's ballpoint pens.

'I would like to buy your idea,' Mr Martin said. 'I could start up a factory in England to make your pens. What do you say? Will you sell me the idea?'

Ladislao Biro did not need to think about Mr Martin's offer for very long. With Mr Martin's money he would be able to

rescue all of his family and bring them safely to Argentina.

He agreed to sell his invention and Mr Martin took the first Biro pen back to England.

Ladislao spent most of the money paying for his relatives to come to safety in Argentina.

Now at last he could relax and enjoy his favourite hobby which was painting.

Henry Martin set up his first factory in England and began to make hundreds of Biro pens.

At this time the airmen who flew in the bombers were having trouble writing on their charts. As an aeroplane flew higher in the sky the air pressure in the plane changed. It seemed to squeeze the little tubes inside their fountain pens and the airmen got many blots of ink on their charts.

Henry Martin asked the Royal Air Force if they would like to try his new ballpoint pens.

They were a great success.

The Royal Air Force used 30,000 Biros. The American Airforce used even more. Naval divers even used them on their charts under water.

The Biro pen was famous. Everyone wanted one.

The very first Biro pen had been sold in Argentina for £25. After the war Henry Martin began to sell Biros in shops in England.

The first pens arrived in the shops in time for Christmas. They cost £2.75 each.

Today the Biro pen is owned by the BIC Company.

The most popular pen is called the BIC Crystal and it costs only fourteen pence. It lasts for two and a half kilometres of writing.

The ink from BIC pens sold every week could draw a line to the sun and back, or go round the earth 8,000 times.

The pens are made with different coloured inks.

Sometimes they have the name of a club or society stamped on them.

Today we take them for granted and when the ink runs out we throw them away.

When Ladislao Biro invented his ballpoint pen with the special quick-drying ink he did not know that it would be used all around the world.

He could not have guessed how it would change the way that we write or that it would help the War effort.

Perhaps if he had been able to set up his own factory he would have been a millionaire today.

We don't know if Ladislao was sorry that he sold his idea to Henry Martin, but he would have been happy to know that his pens became famous all over the world.

Louis Braille
Reading for the Blind

A · B : C ∴ D ∷

E · F ∷ G ∷ H ∷

I · J ∴ K : L :

Two hundred years ago horses were used for transport. Wherever horses were needed, so too were the blacksmith and the harness-maker.

The Braille family lived in France. The town they lived in was called Coupvray. It was just south of Paris.

Monsieur Braille was a harness-maker.

His small son was called Louis. Louis loved to watch his father work. He liked to watch him cut and sew the leather.

The workshop was full of pleasant smells. He loved the smell of the leather, the saddle soap and polish.
It was Louis's sense of smell which would help him when he grew up.

One day Louis's father was talking to a customer. Louis looked at all the shiny tools lying on the bench. He longed to have a go with them, but he knew he wasn't allowed to. Perhaps he would have just one quick go!

He picked up the sharp tool called an awl. It was used to make holes in leather.

He found a piece of leather. He tried to stick the awl into it. It was very tough. The awl slipped and went into his eye.

His parents rushed to get the doctor but Louis's eye was badly damaged. Six months after the accident he lost the sight of both his eyes.

It was hard for Louis to understand that he would never see again. He became sad and lonely.

In those days blind people were treated very badly. No one wanted them. They often had to beg for food. Some even had to work in funfairs where people poked and prodded them. They stumbled about because they could not see, while everyone laughed.

Louis was lucky because his parents loved him. They tried to cheer him up but he thought there was nothing good in his life now.

The family knew a priest called *Abbé* Palluy. The *Abbé* felt sorry for Louis.

Sometimes he took Louis out into the country. They would listen to the birds singing. Louis could smell the hay and the wild flowers. *Abbé* Palluy also read bible stories to him.

'Louis, you must not feel so sad,' *Abbé* Palluy said to him one day. 'There are many things you can do. You can hear the birds and music. You can touch things. You can smell everything. Best of all you can remember what the world was like before your accident. You are not useless because you are blind.'

Louis thought about this. The priest was right. He began to cheer up.

His parents sent him to a school for blind children. It was the only school for blind children in the whole of France.

The school was horrible. It was cold and damp and the children were very miserable.

Louis tried hard to learn to read. The books had big raised letters and it was difficult trying to work out what the words were. Many of the children gave up.

Sometimes the teacher set out some twigs in the shape of letters. This was even harder.

The teacher also made the children remember everything. They had to remember all their spellings and tables. Even the stories that the teacher had told them. If they forgot anything they got into trouble.

Louis Braille knew that this was not a good way to teach children.

As he grew older he began to think of better ways to help blind children. Perhaps they needed a special alphabet of their own?

He tried to make wooden blocks with letters on them but they didn't work.

One day Louis was sitting in a café. He often went there to meet his friends and have coffee.

On this day he met a man called Charles Barbier. Charles had been a captain in Napoleon's army.

The two men talked about Louis's wooden blocks.
Charles was interested.

'I know something you could try,' he said. 'We used it in the
army. It was a way of giving instructions to soldiers at night.
They could not light a torch because the enemy would
have seen the light.'

'What did you do?' asked Louis.

'I used an awl.'

Louis shuddered as he remembered that it had been an
awl which had damaged his eye.

'I used the awl to make holes like dots and dashes in
pieces of card,' Charles explained. 'When the soldier

turned the card over he could feel the bumps. The men soon learned to read the bumps.'

Louis felt very excited. It was so simple!

That night he began to work out a code for the twenty-six letters of the alphabet. Then he added a code for numbers.

It took a very long time to make a code that would work.

He borrowed one of his father's awls. He had sixty-three cards. They looked like sixty-three dominoes. Each card was for a letter or a number.

In 1834 Louis Braille finished his code.

He was now twenty-five and worked as a teacher at the Blind School.

Louis spent a lot of his own money having special books printed. They were for the blind children he taught.
The books were all written in his code.

Everyone called the code *Braille.*

The children loved Louis. He was kind and patient with them. They soon learned to read the Braille. Louis had set them free from their lonely world of blindness.

A few years later Louis worked out a code for reading music. He enjoyed playing the organ. He wanted blind children to have the chance to play music too.

Louis had spent most of his life in the damp, cold Blind School and he became ill with tuberculosis. He died when he was only forty-three.

But the story did not end there.

An English doctor called Dr Armitage had heard about Louis Braille's work. He wanted to help blind children in England.

He set up a company in London to print Braille books. Later, Braille typewriters were invented too.

Nowadays, of course, there are a lot of Braille magazines and books for blind people.

Louis Braille would be very pleased to know that he had helped millions of blind people to enjoy their lives.

Marie Curie
Radium

Marie Curie was born in 1867. She lived in Warsaw in Poland with her father and mother, her two brothers and two sisters. Her Polish name was Maria Sklodowska. Maria's father and mother were teachers. The family lived in a small flat which was joined onto the school where Maria's mother worked.

After Maria was born the flat seemed much too small for seven people.

Mr Sklodowska heard that there was a flat at the school where he worked.

'It is bigger than this,' he told his wife. 'We will be more comfortable there.'

They moved to the new flat and were very happy. Maria's father was a teacher of maths and science. He made sure that his children worked hard at their lessons. Sometimes at mealtimes he would give the children sums to work out in their heads. Maria loved doing them. She was good at maths. Her brothers hated it.

Maria liked science as well and often talked to her father about it.

Sometimes, on Saturdays, he took her to his schoolroom and showed her some experiments.

These were Maria's happiest days.

But some very sad things were about to happen to the family.

Poland had been at war with Russia and when Maria was six, Russian soldiers marched into Poland. The Russians took over Poland.

It was very frightening. They made everyone speak Russian and they would not let Maria's father be a teacher.
The family even had to move out of the new flat where they had been so happy.

Maria's parents managed to find another flat, but it was small and very damp. Maria had to sleep on the sofa.

Maria had always been small for her age and she was a shy, nervous little girl. Now she felt even more scared and she was often ill.

One day something very sad happened. Maria's mother became ill too.

The children had noticed that she did not cuddle them anymore, or kiss them goodnight. The children were puzzled.

'Mama has a disease called tuberculosis,' their father told them. 'She is very ill.'

'I don't want to get too close to you in case you catch it,' their mother explained.

Tuberculosis is a disease of the lungs which makes it difficult to breathe and makes people cough. A lot of people caught the disease in those days especially if they lived in cold, damp houses.

Maria's mother died and so did her oldest sister, Sofia. It was a very sad time.

Maria longed to make her father happy again.

'Papa,' she said one day, 'I am going to work hard at school. I am going to be top of my class. One day I'm going to be a scientist like you.'

Maria's father smiled.

'It will be very hard,' he said. 'People do not expect girls to want to be educated.'

'Well, I'm going to be different. You'll see!' Maria said.

'I'll help you all I can,' Maria's father promised.

Maria had to do all her lessons in the Russian language. It was difficult at first.

One day she had to stand up in class and recite some Russian for the school inspector.

She felt very frightened. Everyone was frightened of the Russians. Maria spoke the new language very well and the school inspector was pleased. Maria ran home to tell her father how well she had done.

He was very proud of her.

Maria continued to work hard, just as she said she would. She was often top of her class and when it was time for her to leave she was given a gold medal. Now at last she could go to university.

But the Russians would only allow boys to go.

Maria was very disappointed because she had worked so hard.

Maria's sister Bronia had wanted to go to university too, but she had to go to France to do this. Perhaps Maria could go as well? It would be wonderful to go to the Sorbonne in Paris with Bronia. But it would cost a lot of money for two of them.

Maria had to get a job. She became a teacher. She was back in the classroom and she enjoyed being with the children.

But she still wanted to be a scientist.

'I can read all the books you lend me, Papa,' she said one day. 'But I can't do experiments. I need the special equipment. I wish I had a laboratory.'

Her father took a deep breath.

'Josef was telling me about a secret college that has been started here in Warsaw. It would be very dangerous to go there. If you got caught there would be terrible trouble.'

Maria was excited. She did not care about the danger. Josef was her cousin. Perhaps he could arrange for her to go to the college?

Maria began to go to the college at weekends. It was at the top of a large building. The students had hung up a name. They had called the building 'The Museum of Industry and Agriculture'. They hoped the Russians would not guess there was a college inside.

A student always stood guard at the door, just in case.

Maria was very happy. Now she had all the equipment she needed. During the week she went on teaching and saved her pay.

At last, when she was twenty-four, she had saved enough money to go to Paris.

Her sister Bronia was married now and had a baby. Maria went to live with her.

Maria was sad to leave her father and brothers, but if she wanted to be a real scientist she would have to leave Poland.

Maria changed her name to Marie and began to learn the French language.

She loved being at the Sorbonne. She enjoyed studying to be a scientist with other students who talked about science all the time. It was lovely to be with her sister too.

In the autumn Marie found herself a little room of her own. It was at the top of six flights of stairs. In summer it was very hot and in winter it was freezing cold. She had very little money for food or heating, but she did not mind. Being able to study was far more important.

Later that year she met the man she was to marry. His name was Pierre Curie and he too was a scientist. He was tall, with auburn hair and a small beard. He was very kind to Marie and she liked him straightaway.

They were married in 1894, when Marie was twenty-seven. A friend gave them a bicycle each as a wedding present and they spent their honeymoon cycling in the French countryside.

Pierre was Laboratory Chief at the School of Industrial Physics and Chemistry. He did not get paid much, but he could use the laboratory for his own experiments.

Marie worked there with him.

They read a lot about the work of other scientists.
Marie and Pierre were particularly interested in the work of
a scientist called Wilhelm Rontgen. He had been using a
substance which gave off very powerful rays. The rays were
so powerful that they penetrated almost anything, including
the human body. Wilhelm Rontgen had discovered the very
first X-rays.

Everyone was talking about the way X-rays would help
doctors see inside people's bodies.

Wilhelm Rontgen had been using a kind of rock called
uranium.

Pierre and Marie wondered if this strange rock could
produce anything else of use to mankind.

The uranium was mixed in another rock called pitchblende.
Pitchblende was very expensive. It was very difficult to
separate the uranium from the pitchblende. The pitchblende
had to be crushed and dissolved in a large pot.

Marie and Pierre spent many long hours stirring the boiling
pitchblende.

After years of careful work, they discovered two more,
powerful substances. These substances also gave off
powerful rays which Marie and Pierre called radiation.

They named the new substances *radium* and *polonium*.

There was a bad side to their work which they did not fully understand.

Marie and Pierre often felt ill and tired. They could not eat and their hands were covered with sores.

They began to realise that the radiation was getting into their bodies.

If it damaged healthy parts of the body, perhaps it could also damage the sick parts and kill off disease, they thought.

There is an illness called cancer. It makes people very ill. Maybe their radiation could kill the cancer?

Pierre and Marie persuaded doctors to try their new discovery. Soon doctors all over the world were using radium. They used a very small amount carefully and it worked. This became known as Nuclear Medicine.

In 1903 Marie and Pierre were given the Nobel Prize for Physics. The Nobel Prize is one of the highest awards in the world. It is given to people who have done something remarkable. Sometimes it is awarded for writing or medicine. Sometimes for making peace.

Three years later Pierre was walking home through the rain. He had his umbrella up. He felt very tired. There was so much traffic. As he tried to cross the road he slipped and fell. He was trampled by a carter's horse and he was killed.

Poor Marie did not know how to bear it. Her dear husband had also been her best friend. Her only comfort was with her two daughters, Irene and Eve, or her work.

Marie continued to work late every day. She spent a lot of time teaching doctors how to use the new radium. She did so well that in 1911 she was awarded another Nobel Prize. This time it was for Chemistry.

Over the years Marie's body had taken in far too much radiation. She had been working with it for most of her life and she was ill.

Her greatest pleasure now was in the success of her daughters. Irene and her husband Frederick Juliot were also scientists. They won a Nobel Prize, too.

Marie Curie died when she was sixty-four.

From her discoveries we now have nuclear power to make electricity and to drive ships and submarines. Perhaps best of all is the way Marie Curie's work has saved the lives of millions of people.

George Stephenson
The Steam Locomotive

When George Stephenson was a little boy he lived in a tiny cottage near the River Tyne in the village of Wylam, not far from Newcastle.

There were six children in his family and there were lots of children in the houses nearby.

George's family was very poor.

The cottage they lived in belonged to Mr Christopher Blackett. Mr Blackett was very rich. He owned most of the land around Wylam. He also owned the coalmine where George's father worked. Many of the village people worked there. It was very hard work and the wages were low.

George's father was in charge of the winding engine. It was a very important job. The engine was in a shed above the mine. It pulled the wagons loaded with coal out of the mine on the end of a long chain.

George loved to go to the mine and watch the engine.

It was very noisy in the engine shed. The chains clanked and groaned as they were wound round a huge wheel. The winding engine hissed and thumped.

George used to take his father's lunch to him. He walked along the wooden track to the engine shed. Sometimes he had to jump out of the way when the chains tightened. That meant that the heavy wagons loaded with coal were on their way up from the mine.

George longed to be old enough to work in the engine shed.

When he was eight, his family moved. George's father had got a job at a coalmine called Dewly Burn.

George was old enough to start work now. He went to work for a lady called Grace Ainslie who owned a farm. He had to look after her cows and stop them from wandering onto the wagon track from the coalmine.

Sometimes he hoed turnips. Sometimes he had to lead the plough horses.

George became very fond of horses.

Horses worked very hard at the mine. They were used to drag wagons of coal up a track called a tramway. At the top of the hill the wagons were emptied. They rolled back down the hill by themselves.

When he was nine George's father told him that he had got him a job at the Dewly Burn mine.

'You are going to be a picker , like your brother James. You will have to pick out all the bits of stone from the buckets of coal,' he explained.

It sounded very boring. George wanted to work on an engine like his father.

Later George got another job at the Black Callerton coalmine nearby.

He found himself working with horses again.

He had to lead them round and round a huge kind of drum called a 'gin'. Ropes were tied to buckets of coal deep in the mine. These were wound over pulley wheels and then round the 'gin' above ground. All day long the horses walked round in a circle to bring the buckets up from the mine.

George felt sorry for them.

'If only there could be an engine to do their work,' he said to himself.

When George was seventeen he finally got work with his father at the Newburn coalmine about two miles away.

At last he could work on an engine. This engine was a pumping engine. It pumped water up from the mine.

He and his father had to keep the pump working so that the mine wouldn't flood. It was a very important job.

George was fascinated by the engine. He loved taking it to bits and cleaning it.

Soon he knew more about the engine than his father did.

He was sure that an engine could be made to do even more work. Perhaps it could be made so that it could travel along? Perhaps it could be used to pull wagons full of people as well as wagons full of coal? He was very excited about this idea. People would be able to travel all over the country. Horses wouldn't have to work so hard.

He wished he could write his ideas down, but he had never been to school. He had always had to work, like other poor children.

George made up his mind. He would go to school. But he was nearly eighteen by the time he could afford the four pence a week to pay for his lessons.

When he started school he realised he knew nothing at all. He even had to learn how to hold a pencil. It was very hard.

But, by the time he was twenty, he had learned to read and write quite well.

Soon afterwards George met a girl called Frances Henderson. He liked her very much and, on 28 November 1802, they were married. The next year they had a baby son. They called him Robert, after George's father.

For a while they were very happy, but then Frances became ill with tuberculosis. She had a cough and she couldn't breathe properly. Frances died in 1805.

George was heartbroken. He needed to get away for a while. He found a kind lady to look after the baby and he went to Scotland. He worked at a coalmine in a place called Montrose.

There were many accidents in coalmines in those days. When George returned home there was more bad news. His father had been hurt and was blind.

George had to work to help his family.

He soon found another job. He worked hard and tried to save some money. One day he would build his own engine.

George became so good at mending engines that soon everyone had heard about him.

He was offered the job of chief engineer at Killingworth coalmine near Newcastle.

Now at last he could begin to work on his own engine. It had to be one which would make wheels turn round. It had to move.

It would be very heavy. He would need iron rails. The wooden ones would not be strong enough.

George worked on his engine at night.

It had a fire box where it burned coal to heat the water.
The boiling water made steam. The steam drove the wheels
round.

He was very proud of the engine and he named it *Blutcher*
after a famous Prussian general. He had spelled the name
wrongly but no one seemed to notice.

The new engine moved along at about 6 kilometres an
hour on the new iron rails George had made for it. It could
pull eight wagons.

Young Robert was very proud of his father. He had just
started going to Dr Bruce's school in Newcastle.

George had bought him a donkey so that he could ride to school.

Robert began to teach his father some of the things he learned at school.

He showed him how to draw plans. This made designing engines easier.

One day George heard that some mine owners at Darlington wanted their coal taken to Stockton on Tees.

They planned to lay a new wooden track for horses to pull the wagons along.

'I can do better than that,' George told the mine owners. 'I can build a locomotive to pull the wagons, but you will have to build an iron track instead of a wooden one.'

The mine owners looked interested.

Then George said, 'We could put more wagons on the back so that people could travel by locomotive too.'

The mine owners were worried. The idea was frightening.

'People would be too scared,' they said.

'Only at first,' George assured them, 'Soon they will realise that it is a good way to travel.'

But the people were frightened.

A locomotive would make too much noise. It would scare the farm animals. The sparks from its chimney might set the crops on fire.

Stage-coach owners were also worried. If travel by locomotive became popular no one would travel in their stage coaches any longer.

The iron rails were laid down. George worked on the new engine which he called *Locomotion.*

On 27 September 1825 the very first steam railway train set off from Darlington.

It was pulling thirty trucks of coal, and a wagonload of very nervous people.

A huge crowd had gathered to watch.

What a noise the train made! Smoke and sparks flew out of its chimney. Clouds of steam covered the crowd with a foul damp mist.

Everyone thought the passengers were very brave, but the passengers said they had enjoyed themselves.

The train had travelled to Stockton on Tees at twelve kilometres an hour.

The mine owners were delighted.

George had never been happier.

He began to build an even better steam engine which he called the *Rocket.*

In 1829 the *Rocket* won £500 in a competition for an engine to run between Liverpool and Manchester.

It would carry cotton to the mills. The new engine made the nineteen-kilometre journey in fifty-three minutes. It was a huge success.

By now Robert had become a fine engineer too. He and his father designed tunnels and embankments for their railways. Trains could not get up and down slopes. They had to have flat ground.

Thousands of men worked on the building of the railway tracks. Soon there were railways all over Britain.

George Stephenson's dream had come true and travel had changed for ever.

George Stephenson's *Rocket* can be seen in the Science Museum in London.

Wilbur and Orville Wright
Powered Flight

This is the story of two boys and an aeroplane. The boys' names were Wilbur and Orville Wright. They lived in a place called Dayton in America. They had two brothers and a sister.

Their father was a bishop. He believed that children should earn their pocket money. To do this they had to help around the house. They also had to make up their own games.

Mrs Wright was the daughter of a wagonmaker. She was good at making things. Once she helped the children to build sledges for playing in the snow.

Mrs Wright taught Wilbur and Orville about machines.

They first became interested in model aeroplanes when their father gave them a toy helicopter.

It was nothing like the toys children play with today. It was made of bamboo and paper and its propeller worked by twisting a rubber band.

Orville was interested in the way the propeller could make toys move. He was also fascinated by kites. He wanted to know what made them rise in the air and which shapes were the best.

He made a fine one for Wilbur. All his friends wanted one so Orville began to sell his kites.

The Wright boys were not only good at making things. They were good business people too. They began to invent ways of printing. Soon they had a small printing business in their shed. They printed leaflets and posters there after they got home from school.

About that time the bicycle was becoming fashionable. It was nothing like the mountain bikes of today, or the racing bike on which Chris Boardman won his Olympic Gold Medal in 1992.

The first bicycles were very uncomfortable. Wilbur and Orville thought that they could design a better bicycle. It would be more interesting than printing.

They began by mending bicycles in their workshop.

Soon they had enough money to begin to build their own bicycle.

They named their first bicycle *Van Cleeve*. This was the name of one of their ancestors who had emigrated from Holland to America many years before. Unfortunately he had been killed by Red Indians so the boys thought the new bicycle would be a kind of memorial to him.

However, the boys soon got bored with their bicycles. They had read a lot about other people's experiments with flying machines. Wilbur and Orville were grown up now. They wanted to design a flying machine of their own.

For hundreds of years people had been trying to copy the way birds flew, but no one had been successful.
Some people made wings to strap to their arms and tried jumping off bridges. Others strapped themselves to double-winged kites or ran from the tops of hills.
Many people died trying to fly.

The two young men had read about the work of a German experimenter called Otto Lilienthal. They were very impressed by his ideas, but he was killed in a crash landing in 1896.

They began to realise that if an aeroplane was to carry a person it would need power. It would also need a way of controlling it. It was dangerous simply waiting for the plane to crash to the ground.

The Wright brothers had also been studying birds.
They were beginning to understand how a bird uses its wings to rise into the air. They spent hours making drawings and finally began to build a bi-plane. This is a plane with two sets of wings, one above the other.

The bi-plane had no engine. It was flown like a large kite, and operated by strings attached to its wings. It also had a flap at the back to control the way it moved up and down.

It was only two metres wide and was therefore too small to carry a person.

They would need to build a much larger plane to be able to carry someone. Perhaps as much as six metres wide.

The brothers set to work but they soon realised that a plane of this size would need plenty of space and a steady wind to lift it, so they wrote to a journalist called Octave Chanute. Octave Chanute was interested in engineering. He had written several articles about people who tried to design aeroplanes.

He wrote back suggesting that they took their plane to a place called Kitty Hawk.

It was a lonely place on the edge of the Atlantic Ocean. There would be lots of space there and plenty of wind, and soft sand dunes to land on.

But it was a very long way away. At least four hundred miles, and on a narrow bit of land that jutted out into the sea.

How could they get their plane there?

They had to take it to pieces and pack it in boxes.

Wilbur set off with it. He travelled by train and boat, and when he arrived he had to find somewhere to stay.

A man called Bill Tate rented him a room in his house and his wife lent Wilbur her sewing machine.

Wilbur set to work to sew the wings using a very strong cotton material similar to that used for the sails of boats.

There was a lot of material.

Next Wilbur put up a big tent on the sand and fixed it securely. He put the plane back together inside the tent.

Orville arrived to help him and they prepared for their test flight.

They waited for a windy day which would help the plane to take off.

One morning they woke up and heard the wind rattling the windows. They dressed excitedly and ran down to the sand. They dragged the plane from the tent and Orville had the first go.

He lay on the lower wing with his head facing forward. He stretched out so that he could reach the controls.

It worked!

The plane rose up into the air and flew a little way. Wilbur ran along beside it cheering and shouting.

The plane worked well and they made many more flights on it. Sometimes they fell off when the wind was strong but they were flying over sand so they were not hurt.

The two young men were thrilled with their plane, but they knew they could make it even better. It was no use if it could only be used in the wind and fell to the ground when the wind stopped.

They needed to build a plane with an engine.

They wanted it to be useful and not simply a toy.

If the plane had an engine the engine could drive the propeller round. The propeller would make the wind and the plane would lift into the air.

Wilbur and Orville packed everything up and put it in a shed they had built that summer. Then they went back to Dayton.

There were weeks of work ahead of them but Wilbur and Orville hardly noticed the time.

The engine began to take shape.

It had a radiator to keep it cool and this was painted black. It was the only paint on the whole aeroplane because even the weight of the paint was important.

There was a two-litre petrol tank with a little valve. The pilot could control the speed by turning the valve.

On the back of the aeroplane there were two propellers. They were connected to the engine by a set of chains, rather like those on bicycles.

Wilbur and Orville even carved the propellers themselves to get exactly the right shape.

The plane had no wheels. It stood on skids. The brothers had made a twenty-metre track for it to slide down.

Wilbur and Orville finished their new plane at last.
They called it the *Flyer*.

It was the autumn of 1903 and they had been working on the *Flyer* for weeks.

They went back to Kitty Hawk with the new plane packed in boxes.

Wilbur and Orville found that their shed had been smashed by storms. They had to mend it and put up a new tent. They were worried because the weather was getting so cold.

On 17 December everything was ready. They got up early and dressed in their best suits. They wore white shirts and starched collars, ties and bowler hats.

They were a little nervous, but very excited.

Some men from the Life Saving Station came to watch. They brought a young boy with them.

At last the moment had come.

Wilbur and Orville tossed a coin to see which of them would fly. Orville won.

He took off his bowler hat and pinned on his flying cap. Then he shook hands with his brother.

He climbed up onto the lower wing and lay down on it. He held on with one hand, leaving the other free to work the new controls.

'Ready!' he shouted. 'I'm starting the engine now!'

The engine clattered into life. The propeller began to spin. The plane moved down the greased rail.

Faster and faster it went, then suddenly it rose in the air. It was about three metres above the ground, heading due north into the wind. Wilbur ran after it shouting encouragement, but his voice was lost in the wind.

It travelled about 36 metres in twelve seconds. Then it crashed onto the sand. One of the skids was cracked.

Orville quickly turned the petrol off.

Everyone clustered round to congratulate him.

It was the first time that an aeroplane had made a controlled, powered flight.

They mended the skid and Wilbur made the second flight. He flew for about 53 metres.

Then Orville had another turn.

The fourth flight was the best when Wilbur flew the plane for 244 metres before it came down again.

It was the most wonderful day of their lives.

They were so happy that they walked all the way across the sand dunes to Kitty Hawk Weather Station. There they sent a telegram to their parents. Their family would be as excited as they were.

The Wright brothers spent the rest of their lives working on aeroplanes. They built bigger and better planes, and taught other pilots how to fly.

They even took their planes by boat across the Atlantic Ocean to show people in France, England and Italy.

They had become very famous.

On 2 August 1909 one of their planes was approved for use with the army.

Three years later a very sad thing happened. Wilbur died of a fever called typhoid. The wonderful partnership was broken.

Their *Flyer* was brought to London to be put on show in the Science Museum.

When the Second World War started in 1939 the plane was taken to pieces and stored in a coalmine for safety.

It returned to America when Orville died and it is now on show in a famous museum in Washington called the Smithsonian Institute.

The Wright brothers changed the world when they invented the first powered aeroplane.

Because of their work we now have Concorde and the Space Shuttle and millions of people fly every year.

Some More Inventors

Charles Babbage 1792–1871
Charles Babbage was an English mathematician who built a mechanical calculating machine called an analytical engine. His ideas formed the basis for electronic computers

John Logie Baird 1888–1946
John Logie Baird was a Scottish inventor who first demonstrated television in 1926. He opened the first television studio in 1929

Karl Benz 1844–1929
Karl Benz was a German engineer who invented the first practical motor car that was powered by an internal combustion engine

Wallace Carothers 1896–1937
Wallace Carothers was an American chemist who discovered nylon, the first man-made polymer fibre to be widely used

Louis Daguerre 1787–1851
Louis Daguerre was a French painter who invented the first practical photographic process

John Dunlop 1840–1921

John Dunlop was a Scottish veterinary surgeon who invented the first air-filled (pneumatic) tyre

George Eastman 1854–1932

George Eastman was an American businessman who, in 1888, invented the first flexible roll film for use in the first Kodak camera. Until then, photographs were taken on glass plates

Thomas Edison 1847–1931

Thomas Edison was an American scientist who produced more than 1,000 inventions. He invented the light bulb and the phonograph, which was the first record player

Alexander Fleming 1881–1955

Alexander Fleming was a Scottish scientist who discovered penicillin

Johannes Gutenberg 1400–1468

Johannes Gutenberg was a German printer who introduced the first printing press into Europe

Edward Jenner 1749–1823

Edward Jenner was a British doctor who in 1796 performed the first successful inoculations against disease

Hans Lippershey 1570–1619

Hans Lippershey was a Dutch spectacle maker who invented the telescope

Auguste Lumière 1862–1954
Louis Lumière 1864–1948

Auguste and Louis Lumière were French inventors who developed the movie camera and colour photography. They were the first people to open a public cinema. The first film was shown in it in 1895

Guglielmo Marconi 1874–1937

Guglielmo Marconi was an Italian inventor who developed the first radio transmitters and receivers. In 1901 he transmitted the first radio signals across the Atlantic

Samuel Morse 1791–1872

Samuel Morse was an American inventor who developed the electric telegraph in the USA and invented Morse code

Alfred Nobel 1833–1896

Alfred Nobel was a Swedish chemist who invented dynamite. He founded the Nobel prizes which are given to people for achievement in physics, chemistry, medicine, literature and world peace

Joseph Priestly 1733–1804

Joseph Priestly was an English scientist who discovered oxygen in 1774. He was also the inventor of the first fizzy drink

Sir Frank Whittle 1907–

Sir Frank Whittle, an English inventor and aviator who invented the jet engine